Joanna Cole

A Snake's Body

photographs by Jerome Wexler

A TRUMPET CLUB
SPECIAL EDITION

Published by The Trumpet Club
666 Fifth Avenue New York, New York 10103

Reprinted by arrangement with William Morrow and Company, Inc.
Printed in the United States of America September 1989

10 9 8 7 6 5 4 3 2 1 UPC

For his helpful reading of the manuscript, the author thanks Paul Kelly, teaching fellow, Department of Biology, New York University.

Photo Credits: American Museum of Natural History, 15, 18-19, 32; New York Zoological Society, 46, 47, 48.

If you see an animal that has no legs and whose body is many, many times longer than it is wide...

And if that animal is a reptile, a cold-blooded, land-dwelling creature covered with scales...

And if that animal never eats any plants, but lives entirely by killing other animals for food...

Then chances are good that you are looking at a snake.

In the pictures here, you can look closely at a single snake. It is a pet Indian python. Pythons are constrictors; that is, they kill their prey by squeezing.

Indian pythons are among the six largest kinds of snakes in the world. They can grow to be twenty feet long and weigh two hundred pounds. They are known as giant snakes.

The snake shown here is still young. It is a year and a half old, is about six feet long, and weighs only six pounds.

The snake's body looks as if it is all one piece, but part of it is actually the tail. The arrow shows the narrow place where the body ends and the tail begins.

Inside the snake's long, narrow body, its organs are also long and thin.

Organs that usually come in pairs, like kidneys, lie one in front of the other.

Many snakes have only one very long, thin lung. Pythons have two lungs, but one is much smaller than the other.

In this way, the organs are arranged to fit into the narrow space of the body.

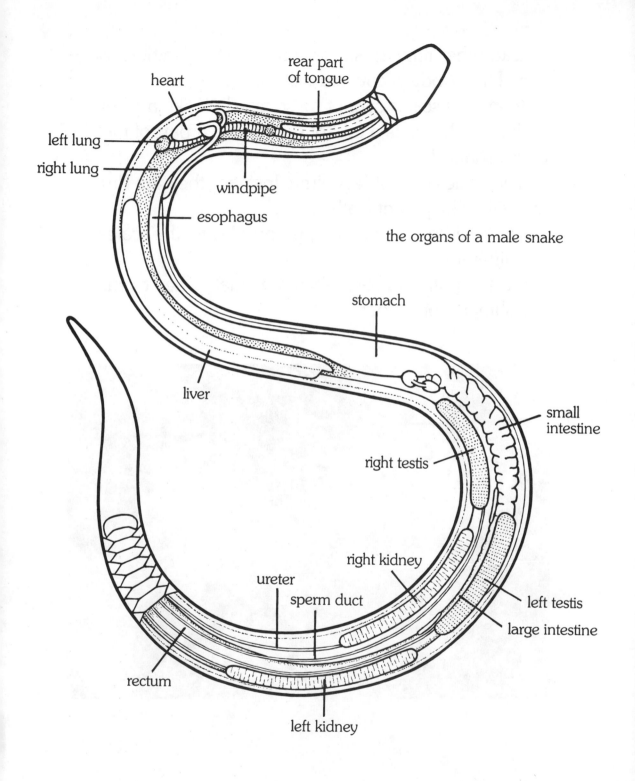

heart

rear part of tongue

left lung

right lung

windpipe

esophagus

the organs of a male snake

stomach

liver

small intestine

right testis

right kidney

ureter

sperm duct

left testis

large intestine

rectum

left kidney

Like other reptiles, snakes have no fur, feathers, or hair. Their body is covered with scales.

A snake's scales cannot be scraped off like a fish's scales. Each one is a fold of skin and is a part of the entire snakeskin.

The scales do not feel slimy. Instead, they are dry and silky like patent leather.

On different parts of the python's body, the scales are different.

On the python's back, they are small. They overlap like shingles on a roof.

The belly scales are large and flat. Scales of this size are called "plates." Each belly plate matches up with a pair of ribs inside the snake's body.

The last belly plate before the tail is larger than the others. It is the anal scale. It covers the snake's cloaca, the opening where body wastes pass out.

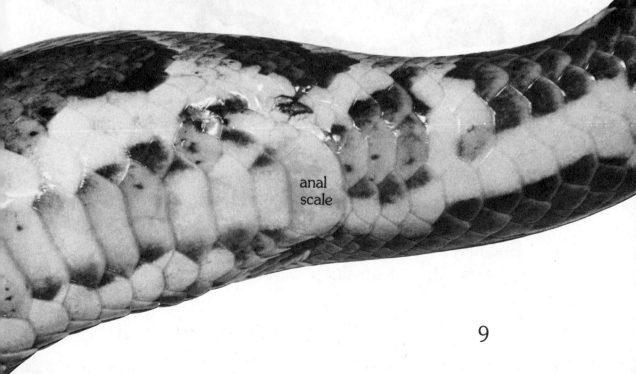

anal scale

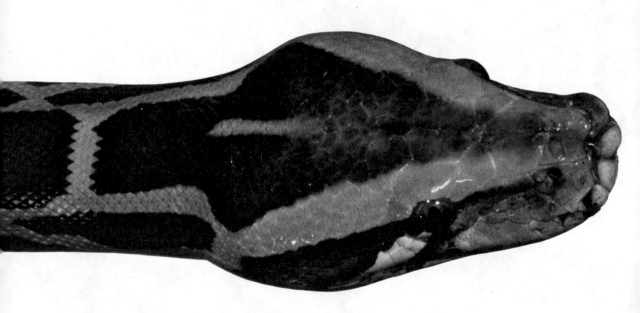

The plates on the head are all different sizes. They form a pattern. Even the snake's eye is covered by a scale. It is round and clear like a built-in contact lens. It protects the eye from dirt and scratches.

Because snakes have no eyelids, they cannot close their eyes. They even sleep with their eyes wide open!

Under the snake's outer skin, a new set of scales is always growing. When the new skin is ready, the snake sheds its old skin. This shedding is called "molting."

The first sign that the snake is going to molt is that the skin becomes dull and milky in color. Even the eye scale clouds over. The python's eyes stay cloudy for about eight days. During that time, the snake is partly blind.

About three or four days after the eyes clear up, the python begins to molt.

First it makes tears in the skin around its lips by rubbing against rough objects. Then it strips off the skin by crawling against the ground or by passing through narrow places. As the skin comes off, it turns inside out, like a sweater.

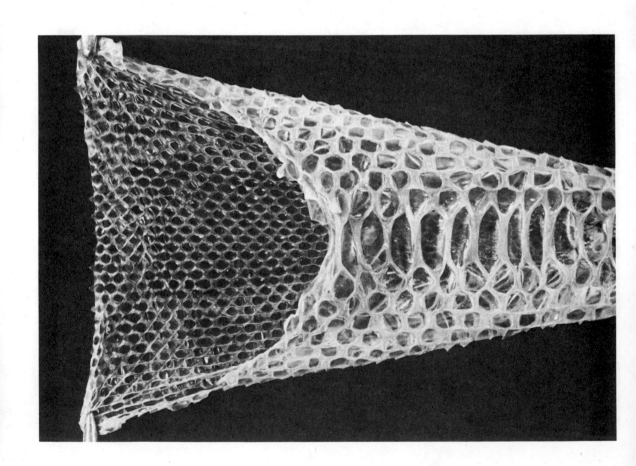

In these two pictures you can see the shed skin. The pattern of the belly plates, the head plates, and the eye scales shows up clearly.

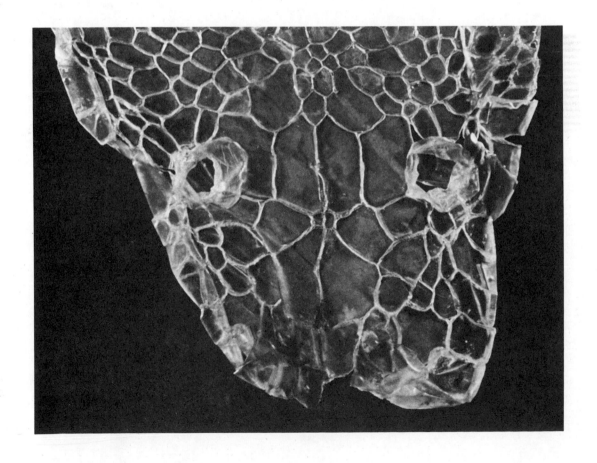

Since snakes are cold-blooded animals, they must get almost all their heat from outside the body. A snake makes a little bit of heat by digesting food, but this amount is not enough to keep its body temperature up.

Small reptiles can raise their temperature quickly, even when the air is cool, by basking in the sun. But basking would take too long for a large, heavy snake. Perhaps for this reason all the giant snakes, including pythons, live in tropical climates where the air stays warm.

A small reptile can raise its temperature
above the air temperature by basking in the sun.

Probably the first thing that one notices about snakes is that they have no legs. Scientists think that the ancestors of snakes were prehistoric lizards. When snakes came into being millions of years ago, they gradually lost their limbs. Today most snakes have nothing left at all of the lost legs.

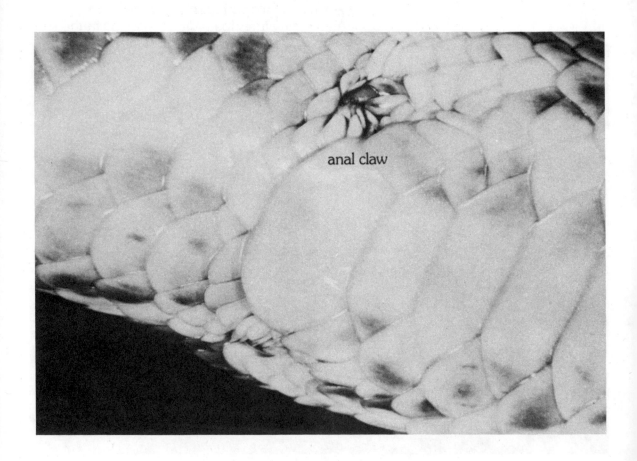

anal claw

But pythons have two claws, one on each side of the anal scale, that show where the hind legs used to be.

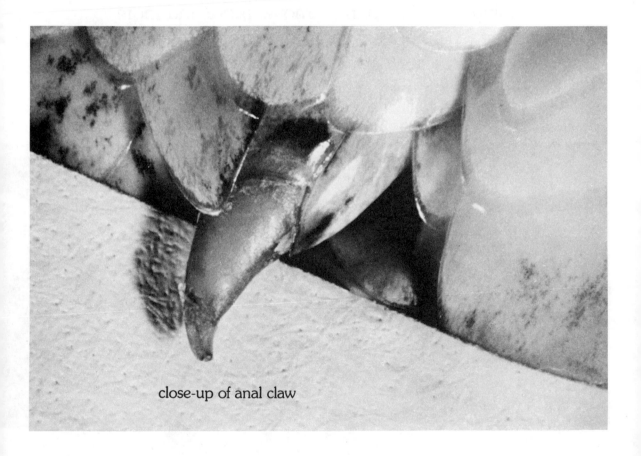

close-up of anal claw

If an animal like a dog or cat suddenly lost its legs, it would be helpless. It could hardly move, and it certainly could not catch healthy, fast-moving prey.

As snakes lost their limbs, however, they gained something else to help them move: more and more vertebrae (spine bones) and more and more ribs. The largest snakes today may have as many as four hundred sets of ribs.

skeleton of a python

The snake's long and flexible spine allows it to turn and twist almost into knots. This ability to twine is the secret of moving without legs.

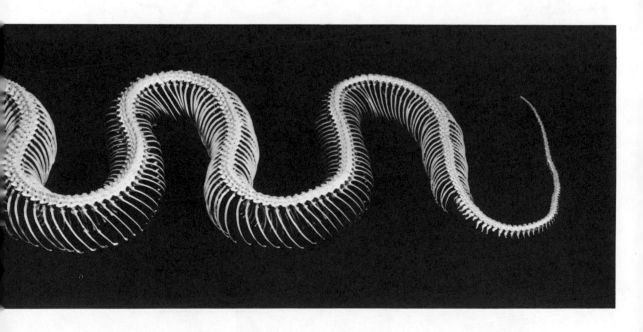

Snakes have four different ways of moving:

1. Moving in waves (or undulatory movement):
Most snakes move this way most of the time. They slither forward by making wavy motions with their long body. Every part of the body follows the same path as the head.

The belly plates press against rocks, branches, or rough ground and push the snake along. When swimming, the same waving movements push the body against the water and move the snake forward.

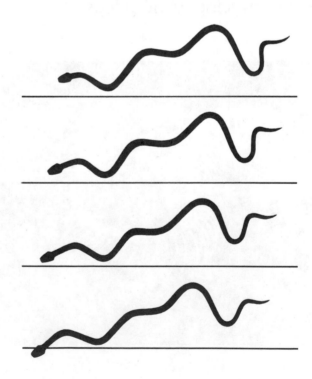

2. Concertina movement:

When a snake goes through a narrow space, or when it climbs a tree, its body acts like a concertina, or small accordion.

The snake grips the surface with the scales on the underside of the head and pulls the rest of the body up in loops. Then it grips with the tail, shoves the front forward, and repeats the action again.

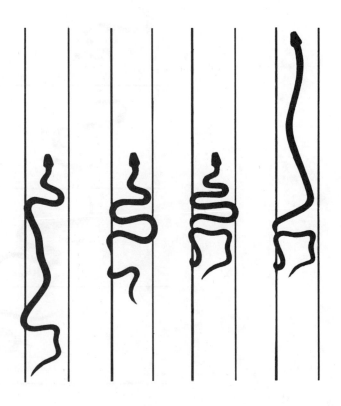

3. Sidewinding:

Some desert snakes move sideways. Instead of slithering forward with the belly on the ground, they lift the body in loops and take "steps" with small areas on the underside of the body. This way of moving helps the snake get a grip in shifting sand and keeps most of the belly away from the burning heat of the surface.

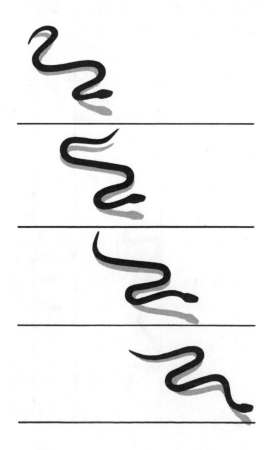

4. Caterpillar movement:

Heavy-bodied snakes like pythons often use this sluglike crawl. The body stays straight. One group of belly plates is pulled forward across the ribs by muscles, and the back edges of the plates grip the ground like tractor treads. Then the next group of belly plates moves. The whole process looks like a ripple of skin passing along the underside of the snake.

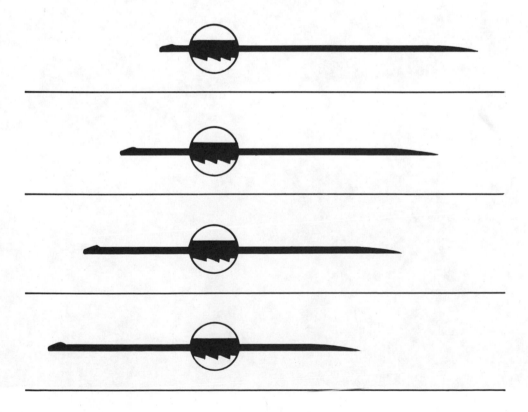

This close-up picture of the shed skin shows how the belly plates are pleated at the back edge. The pleats allow the scales to pull away from the body slightly and get a grip on the ground when the snake moves.

The snake's four ways of moving make it an excellent hunter. In the jungle, where vegetation is dense, legs might get in the way. But even a very large python can slide silently through small spaces and come upon prey without warning.

Pythons also have special senses that help them capture prey. But the two senses that are most important to human beings—sight and hearing—are not the most important to a snake.

Snakes do not have much sense of hearing. As you can see from the picture, they have no outside ears, and they have no eardrums inside either. They can pick up vibrations from the ground or from approaching storms, but they cannot hear sounds the way human beings do.

And, although the snake's eyes are always open, its vision is not very good. It probably sees the way you do out of the corner of your eye. It senses movement, but does not see objects clearly.

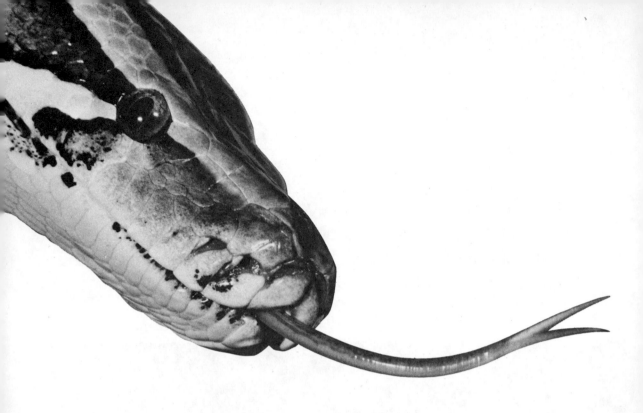

The snake's most important sense is its sense of
smell. But here is a surprise. The snake smells with its
tongue. There are very few taste buds on the tongue,
so apparently a snake does not taste much. But it flicks
its tongue in and out of the mouth constantly, testing
the air for smells.

The tips of the forked tongue pick up gases from the
air. Then the tongue is pulled back into the mouth,
and the tips are stuck into two holes in the roof of the
mouth. These holes lead to Jacobson's organ, a special
organ of smell.

Here you can see how the snake can stick out its tongue without opening its mouth. The tongue darts in and out of a notch in the upper lip.

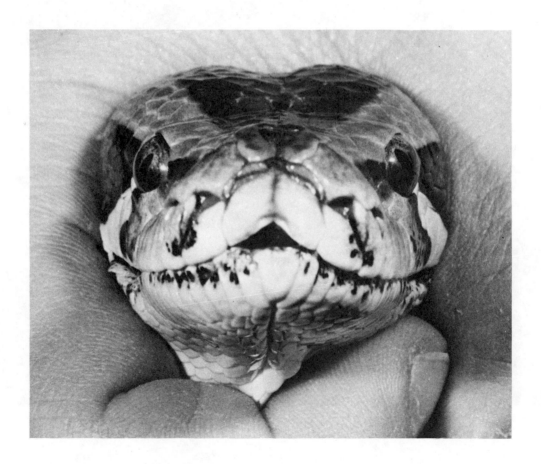

When it is not being used, the tongue is pulled into a sheath in the mouth. This sheath is also the beginning of the snake's windpipe.

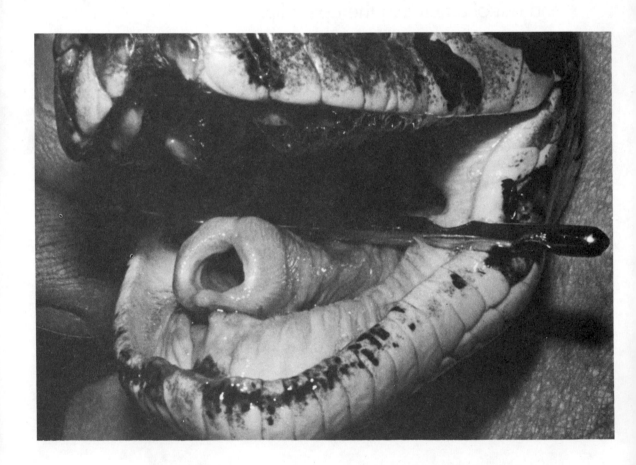

A python has one more sense that most other animals do not have. It is a heat detector.

On the python's upper lips are pits, or little holes. In the holes are organs that detect heat radiations in the air. The python can sense a warm animal nearby.

Using its keen sense of smell and its heat organs, a python can hunt easily in the dark or in the jungle, where prey may be close by but hidden from sight by leaves.

Arrows show the heat pits on the snake's lip.

After a snake has detected prey with its senses, it captures and kills it.

Poisonous snakes inject a poison called "venom" into the prey through special teeth called "fangs." Then they wait until the animal dies before eating it.

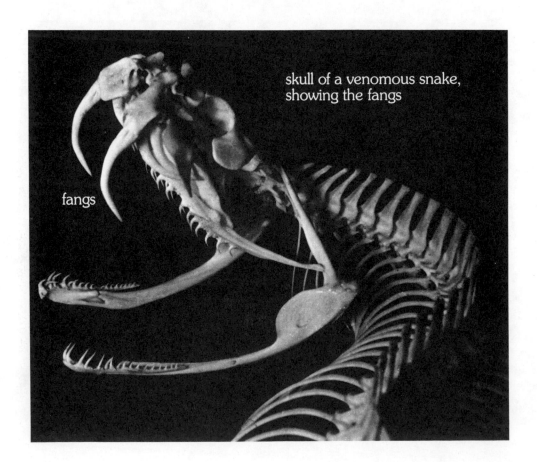

skull of a venomous snake, showing the fangs

fangs

A python is not a venomous snake, so it does not have fangs. It is a constrictor. To kill prey, it must catch and hold the animal with its teeth. Then it can squeeze it to death in the coils of its body.

The python's back-curving teeth help to keep the prey from escaping; the harder an animal pulls out, the farther in the teeth will go.

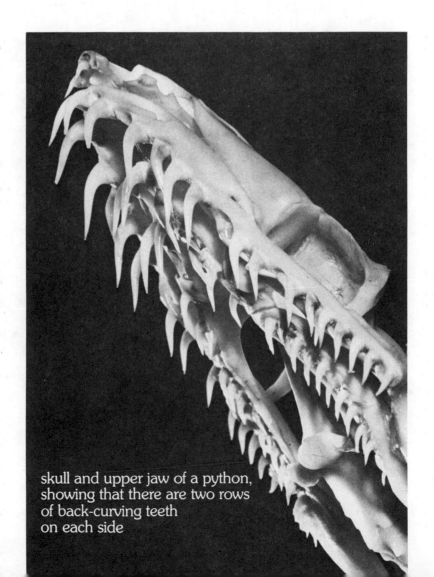

skull and upper jaw of a python, showing that there are two rows of back-curving teeth on each side

The pet python is usually fed freshly killed rats, frogs, and chicks.

In the following pictures, you can see how it goes about killing and eating a live animal.

First the snake senses the presence of the chick and approaches it.

Then it uses its teeth to grasp the prey.

Still holding onto the chick with its mouth,
the snake starts to throw a coil around it.

Now the coil is wrapped around the chick
and tightened…

until the breath is squeezed out.

In a few seconds, the chick is still.

Now the snake loosens its coil.
It begins looking for the chick's head,
which it will swallow first.

Still using its body to hold the prey,
the snake takes the chick into its mouth.

Strangely, the narrowest of animals—the snake—
must swallow its food in the biggest pieces. Snakes
cannot bite off chunks of their prey. Instead, they must
swallow it whole.

To do so, the snake's jawbones can stretch apart,
allowing the prey to go down.

The python has no trouble swallowing the chick, and if it had to, it could swallow an object four or five times as wide as its head.

The snake's stomach and skin can also stretch to hold a big meal. The arrow shows the bulge the chick's body makes as it passes down the python's throat.

Because the snake can swallow such large prey, it can eat about four hundred times its daily food needs in one meal. Snakes can go without food for over a year, although they usually eat every week or so.

After the snake has digested its food, the waste materials pass through the cloaca. The dropping is made up of three parts: One is dark brown and is like the dung of many other animals. A whitish-gray part is mainly uric acid and could be thought of as solid urine. Although the snake drinks water, it has no urine bladder and does not urinate.

The third part of the dropping is a ball of hair, feathers, or fur, which the snake cannot digest.

The quarter shows the size of the snake's droppings.

In order to survive as a species, snakes must bear young.

After mating with a male python, the female lays from fifteen to a hundred eggs. Larger pythons lay more eggs, and smaller ones lay fewer eggs.

After laying them, she draws them together in a pile. She wraps her body around them and rests her head on top.

The female python is the only snake that can raise its own body temperature. She does so only when she is hatching her eggs. Her muscles quiver rapidly and make heat. In this way, the female python can raise her temperature about 7 degrees Celsius higher than the air around her.

For as long as six weeks, the mother snake stays coiled around her eggs. She is keeping them warm, more like a bird than a reptile. She gets off them only a few times to drink. Then, before the eggs hatch, she leaves them.

When the young snakes come out of the leathery eggs, they are already able to care for themselves. At first, they do not need to eat. For a few days, they use up the food they absorbed while still in the egg.

Each baby is smaller than its parents, about two feet long. And it cannot yet mate or lay eggs. But, in every other way, its body and habits are just the same as an adult's. Almost at once it begins to live like any other python, using its special body to capture the prey on which it lives.